TAO TE CHING

TAO TE CHING
LAO-TZU

TRANSLATED BY
Stephen Addiss and
Stanley Lombardo

INTRODUCTION BY
Burton Watson

INK PAINTINGS BY
Stephen Addiss

Shambhala
Boulder
2007

Shambhala Publications, Inc.
4720 Walnut Street
Boulder, Colorado 80301
www.shambhala.com

19 18 17 16 15 14 13 12 11

Printed in the United States of America

Interior design and composition: Greta D. Sibley & Associates

♾ This edition is printed on acid-free paper that meets the American National Standards Institute z39.48 Standard.

♻ This book is printed on 30% postconsumer recycled paper. For more information please visit www.shambhala.com.

Shambhala Publications is distributed worldwide by Penguin Random House, Inc., and its subsidiaries.

Library of Congress Cataloging-in-Publication Data
Laozi.
[Dao de jing. English]
Tao te ching/Lao-Tzu; translated by Stephen Addiss and Stanley Lombardo; introduction by Burton Watson; ink paintings by Stephen Addiss.
p. cm.
ISBN 978-1-59030-546-1 (alk. paper)
I. Addiss, Stephen, 1935–   II. Lombardo, Stanley, 1943–   III. Title.
BL1900.L26E5 2007
299.5'1482—dc22
2007015196

CONTENTS

Translators' Preface

vii

A Note on the Calligraphy

xiii

Chinese Pronunciation Guide

xv

Introduction

xvii

Tao Te Ching

I

Glossary of Chinese Words

113

TRANSLATORS' PREFACE

There are already more than one hundred translations of the *Tao Te Ching* into English. Why should this text be translated again? Specifically, what could we do that had not been done before?

After examining previous translations, we came to realize that there were four things we could attempt that were different and potentially useful. First, we wanted to translate rather than explain the text. The *Tao Te Ching* is always terse, and sometimes enigmatic. Previous translators have often offered explications rather than pure translations; they explained what they thought Lao-tzu meant rather than what he said. We have chosen to let the text speak for itself as much as possible.

Second, we found that earlier translations, because they often paraphrase the text, tend to be verbose, extending the concise Chinese text into much longer sentence patterns. To some extent this is inevitable. Chinese consists of a single monosyllable for each word and often does not mark such grammatical features as tense and number. Any intelligible English translation must use more words and syllables than the original text, but we believe that it is possible to recreate much of the terse diction and staccato

rhythm of the ancient Chinese. Therefore we have kept, as much as possible, to the bare bones of the language, favoring Anglo-Saxon monosyllables over Latinate polysyllables. In this way we have tried to preserve some of the flavor of the original text.

Third, we have completely avoided gender-specific pronouns. The original Chinese does not have the pronouns *he* or *she,* but previous translators have inserted *he* to refer to the Taoist Sage. It could be argued that most early Taoists may have been male, but the *Tao Te Ching* often praises the female spirit, and there is no reason why the text does not apply to women as well as to men. Therefore we have been gender neutral in our translation.

Finally, we have provided an interactive element in our translation. Since no version can replace the original text as a document, not only will each generation retranslate and reinterpret the text, but each reader should have some direct contact with the original words. We have therefore provided a transliteration of one line in each section, together with the original Chinese characters, keyed to a glossary.

Our initial task was to decide which version of the *Tao Te Ching* to translate. It may be convenient to believe that every "classic" text is fixed and set, ready to be received in complete and finished form. However, this is seldom if ever the case. *The Tao Te Ching,* for example, has long been known from a text that dates from the first to third centuries C.E., but recently two older versions of the text were discovered in the Mawangdui tomb, of the first century B.C.E. Several recent translations have utilized these

earlier texts, which differ primarily by starting with section 38 rather than with what has been known as section 1. After some consideration, we decided to remain with the slightly later text (known as the Wang Pi text), in part because it has been known and studied first in China and later all around the world for centuries, in part because the Mawangdui texts may have been altered to suit the taste and needs of a governmental leader, and in part because section 1 is clearly a stronger and more convincing opening of the text than is section 38. We believe that starting with the Tao and later coming to the Te fits the internal logic of the text. We have, however, constantly checked and compared the Mawangdui texts and occasionally have utilized them when we felt that they clarified certain passages.

We next began the process of translation itself. This meant studying earlier commentaries and checking every word in terms of meanings and etymology. For example, the word 順 can be translated as "order," but it is actually composed of the graphs for "river" and "head." We therefore translate it as "headwaters." We also discussed with each other the phrasings of both the original Chinese and our new English version. In the process we came across a number of phrases that seemed to us especially significant. In order to make our translation interactive, these are the segments of text we present for each section in Chinese as well as English. This will enable the reader to gain some appreciation of how the Chinese language functions and to arrive at an independent understanding of some of the most significant phrases.

In Chinese, each monosyllabic word is represented by its own character or graph, rather than by letters of an alphabet. Here, for example, are the words in the first line of the text.

道   *Tao* means "way" in both literal ("road") and metaphysical ("spiritual path") senses. It can also, more rarely, mean "to say" or "to tell."

可   *k'o* indicates potential: "possible" or "can be."

非   *fei* is a negative, meaning "no" or "not."

常   *ch'ang* means "common, enduring," lasting, and suggests the reality and constancy of everyday life.

We can now examine the famous first line of the *Tao Te Ching* to see what kinds of problems and possibilites any translator, and in truth any reader, faces when reading this text. The first line has six characters, three of which are the same.

道	可	道	非	常	道
Tao	*k'o*	*tao*	*fei*	*ch'ang*	*tao*

Literally this may be translated word for word:

道	可	道	非	常	道
Way	can be	way/tell	not	enduring/constant	way.

The phrase has been translated in various ways, but usually with the same basic meaning:

The way that can be spoken of is not the constant way. (Lau)
The Way that can be told of is not an Unvarying Way. (Waley)
The tao that can be told is not the eternal tao. (Mitchell)
The Tao that can be told is not the invariant Tao. (Lafargue)
The Tao that can be told of is not the eternal Tao. (Chan)
The Tao that can be told is not the eternal Tao. (Feng and
    English)
The Tao that can be expressed is not the eternal Tao. (Ch'u)
The tao that can be said is not the everlasting tao. (Gibbs)

Two translations avoid the idea of "said" or "told":

The ways that can be walked are not the eternal Way. (Mair)
If Tao can be Taoed, it's not Tao. (Maurer)

In our own case, we first decided that the word *Tao* is
so important, and is now so often used in English, that it
did not need to be translated. Secondly, our version retains
the six monosyllables of the original in order to retain the
simplicity, rhythm, and power of the Chinese:

Tao called Tao is not Tao.

We deliberately delayed words such as "can be" and "enduring" until the second line (which has a parallel con-
struction) in order to make our translation have the impact
of the original. We realize, however, that the other translations cited here, or ones that any reader can make, might
be considered to suit the text as well or better.

Readers are invited to use the glossary given at the end of this translation for all Chinese words given in the text or to consult the famous *Matthews' Chinese-English Dictionary*. In either case the characters may be looked up by their pronunciations in order to study their varieties of meanings. Whichever course the reader takes, the text should be open to interpretation, rather than closed. The challenge, the vexation, and the delight for each translator, and for each reader, is to make the text come alive again for oneself, right here, right now.

—Stephen Addiss and Stanley Lombardo

A NOTE ON THE CALLIGRAPHY

The calligraphy is derived from free versions of significant words of the text, often done in new versions of ancient seal-script characters (1, 21, 22, 41, 47, 63, 66) but sometimes written in modified regular script (11, 40, 68) or simplified cursive script (5, 8, 32, 37, 65, 73) or even in English (81). The ink-paintings (4, 14, 25, 42, 52, 76) are even more freely brushed, suggesting the workings of the Tao in the void through circular and other continuously varied forms.

The style of the art has some affinities with Zen brushwork; since Zen was strongly influenced by Taoism, that is not surprising. Ultimately, however, these are visual expressions of meanings that go beyond words.

CHINESE PRONUNCIATION GUIDE

Unlike English, Chinese is a tonal language, so that a word like *ma* can mean different things depending upon whether it is spoken with a low, high, rising, or falling tone of voice. We might imagine some of this change if we consider the differences in accentuation we might make saying "Ma" "Ma!" "Ma?" and "Maaah." Chinese also has many dialects, and even the standard (Mandarin) pronunciation has given rise to several different systems of romanization. We are using the traditional Wade-Giles system, in which the vowels are pronounced generally as follows:

> *a* as in f*a*ther
> *e* as in th*e* (or *u*nder, or d*u*d)
> *i* as in p*i*n, or as in b*ee*
> *o* as in *o*ld, or as in w*oo*d
> *u* as in y*ou*, or as in c*ou*ld

The consonants are quite similar to English, with two exceptions. *J* is pronounced closer to *r*; and when followed by an apostrophe, *ch*, *k*, *p*, and *t* are aspirated:

ch'ang is pronounced "chahng"
ching is pronounced "jing"
kan is pronounced "gahn"
k'o is pronounced "kuh"
p'ai is pronounced "pah-i" (pie)
ping is pronounced "bing"
tao is pronounced "dah-o" (dow)
t'un is pronounced "tuhn"

Therefore the Chinese title of this book, *Tao Te Ching*, is actually pronounced "Dow Duh Jing."

INTRODUCTION

by Burton Watson

Ancient China

Traditional accounts of Chinese history customarily begin by describing certain ancient rulers such as the Yellow Emperor or Yao and Shun, paragons of virtue and wisdom, who first taught the arts of civilization to the Chinese people. Scholars now agree that in all probability these figures were originally local deities who, in the process known as euhemerism, were in later ages divested of their more blatantly supernatural characteristics and made to look like historical personages.

These mythic figures are followed by the so-called Three Dynasties, the Hsia, the Shang or Yin, and the Chou, which grew out of earlier Neolithic settlements centered around the Yellow River valley in northern China. The first of these, the Hsia, is at present known to us only through later written sources. No indisputable archeological proof of its existence has so far been discovered, although, given the startling finds that are coming to light in China these days, that situation may well change.

Excavations carried out in the early twentieth century have yielded ample evidence of the Shang dynasty which

ruled the Yellow River plain from about 1500 to 1000 B.C.E. Most significant among the Shang period finds are the oracle bones used by Shang diviners in a process by which heat was applied to the bone and the response to the diviner's query read in the cracks that resulted. These bones were often inscribed with notations indicating the question asked and, in some cases, the answer that was received. At present, these oracle-bone inscriptions constitute the earliest known specimens of the Chinese writing system, though their degree of sophistication suggests that they are the product of a long process of development, and in fact a recent archeological find may represent an example of the writing system that dates back many centuries earlier.

The Shang state was overthrown in time and replaced by a people known as the Chou, who had previously resided on its western border. Concerning the Chou dynasty, which was founded around 1045 and lasted until 256 B.C.E., we have abundant information both from written sources and from archeological evidence. Though the customs of the Chou people differed somewhat from those of the Shang, the Chou on the whole carried on the culture and civilization of the preceding dynasty. After completing the conquest of the Shang, the Chou ruler parcelled out the territory under his control to close relatives, men of other clans who had aided him, and to older rulers already established in the area, thus creating a patchwork of little feudal realms or city-states that stretched all across northern China. The lords of these city-states, which were said to number seventy or more, paid tribute to the Chou king, periodically attended his court, and assisted him in

times of war, but were otherwise free to govern their domains as they wished. The lords, like the Chou ruler, lived in walled enclosures, in wooden structures built on foundations of tamped earth. Just outside the walls, in much humbler dwellings, lived the artisans and peasants. In later Chou times a second wall was frequently built to enclose this outer area, thus creating the walled cities that were a hallmark of premodern China.

The Chinese in ancient times referred to themselves as the *Hua*, the "Flowery" or "Splendid" people, a designation that even today constitutes part of the official name of China. They also spoke of their country as *Chung-kuo*, or the Middle Kingdom, picturing themselves as occupying a bright plateau of civilization that sloped off sharply on all sides into barbarian darkness. In these dark outer regions lived various non-Chinese peoples, differing from the Chinese in language and habits and in many cases pursuing a nomadic or hunting and gathering mode of life, in contrast to the overwhelmingly agricultural Chinese.

In an effort to open up new lands for cultivation, the Chinese were continually pushing into the territories of these foreign tribes, spurring them at times to armed resistance. Thus, as in the preceding Shang period, the ruler and his barons were frequently engaged in warfare with enemies abroad or with insurgents within the realm. The nobles rode into battle in horse-drawn chariots and fought with bronze-fitted spears, halberds, and bows and arrows. Foot soldiers, pressed into service from the peasantry, ran alongside the chariots. In times of peace the nobles held elaborate hunts for recreation and as a form of military drill.

In addition to warfare, the aristocrats devoted much time to sacrifices and other religious observances. Sacrifices were offered first of all to the ancestors of the family, who watched over their descendants from their dwelling in the sky and conferred blessings in return. Sacrifices were also offered to various nature deities and to important rivers and mountains. The Chou ruler, referred to as the Son of Heaven, sacrificed to a sky deity known as *T'ien* or Heaven, who was believed to certify his right to rulership through the Mandate of Heaven but, if displeased, could withdraw the mandate and bestow it elsewhere. Wine, grain, fruit, and animal flesh were the usual offerings, proffered to the spirits in ornately decorated bronze vessels. In Shang and early Chou times, human sacrifices were also occasionally performed, the victims usually being prisoners of war who were slain so they could attend the soul of a newly deceased ruler.

To insure the efficacy of these sacrifices, participants had to abide by carefully prescribed rituals, a fact that accounts for the great preoccupation with ritual texts and procedures in ancient Chinese culture. There was no separate priestly class or caste, but the sacrificers were often assisted by professional diviners, invocators, or shamans. The more important sacrifices and other rites were carried out to musical accompaniment, as music was thought to have the power to move the spirits and to exercise a profound moral influence in human affairs. Good music, the Chinese held, insures peace and uprightness; bad music leads to lewdness and social decline.

The Chou rulers originally had their capital far to the west in the Wei River valley, but internal dissent and for-

eign invasion in 771 forced them to move east to Lo-yang, an event that marks the beginning of the Eastern Chou period (771–256 B.C.E.). In the centuries that followed, the actual power of rule gradually passed into the hands of the more important feudal lords, but the Chou kings were permitted to remain as titular sovereigns because of the sanctity of their position and the religious duties that they alone were qualified to perform. Meanwhile, the more powerful feudal states swallowed up one after another of their feebler neighbors until, by the beginning of the Warring States period (403–221 B.C.E.), only seven states remained in existence, locked in a ceaseless struggle for dominance.

By this time warfare had increased greatly in scale and complexity. Through contact with nomadic peoples to the north, the Chinese had learned to ride horseback, and the introduction of iron weapons and new devices such as the crossbow made for more deadly combat. Similar advances such as the introduction of iron farm implements and large-scale irrigation projects had likewise increased agricultural efficiency. Cities grew dramatically in size and complexity, copper coinage came into use, and merchants traveled from state to state peddling staple items and luxury goods.

As the rulers of the larger states annexed the lands and populations of smaller states or pushed back the frontier to open up more areas for cultivation, they faced new problems in administration. Whereas in earlier times the major administrative posts had been the hereditary prerogative of the older noble families within the state, the

rulers now increasingly made such offices appointive and filled them with men selected from the lower ranks of the nobility for their ability and personal loyalty to the ruler. Time-honored rites and customs that had regulated society in the earlier Chou period gave way to bureaucratic methods of administration, older systems of tribute were replaced by regular taxes on land and produce, and all efforts were bent toward achieving the most effective control of population and resources so that the state could survive in the cutthroat tenor of the times and advance its goals.

All these factors led to a dramatic breakdown in old ways of thought and codes of morality and helped to make the period of the Warring States one of the most brilliant and creative in the history of Chinese thought. Challenged by the rapidly shifting conditions of the period and encouraged by prospects of advancement to office, thinkers came forward to offer the rulers of the various states their advice on political and ethical matters, often journeying from state to state in search of a ruler with a sympathetic ear. Out of this intellectual ferment emerged the writings of the so-called Hundred Schools of philosophy, among them the text presented here in translation, the *Lao-Tzu* or *Tao Te Ching*.

The Hundred Schools

The oldest, and in later times perhaps the most influential, of these schools of thought was Confucianism. It

traced its origin to K'ung Fu-tzu or Confucius (551–479 B.C.E.), a member of the lower nobility and a minor official in the small state of Lu, whose prime importance lay in his role as a teacher. Perhaps because of its relatively early origin, Confucianism is in many ways the most conservative of the schools of thought, seeking a return to the customs and values of the early Chou, which it pictured as a golden age, through the study of the ancient texts and rituals and an intense moral dedication. It placed great emphasis on the family, believing that only when moral obligations within the family are properly observed can such values then be extended to embrace the state and society as a whole. It referred often to the concept of Heaven and the rituals relating to the worship of Heaven and the ancestors, but it tended to give such rituals and concepts a strongly humanistic interpretation.

Another school, the Mo-ist, founded by Mo Ti, who flourished in the latter half of the fifth century, resembles Confucianism in its reverence for antiquity and emphasis upon ethical principles. But whereas the Confucians aimed at a graded compassion and concern for others that paid highest respect to parents and close kin, Master Mo called for a universal love encompassing all human beings in equal degree. Like the Confucians, he stressed the role of Heaven and other spiritual beings but portrayed them as dour judges ever ready to intervene in human affairs to reward good and punish evil. Fiercely opposed to the incessant warfare of the times, he is said to have hastened to the aid of states that were under attack in order to discourage aggression, a practice that led later followers of

the school to concern themselves with techniques of defensive warfare.

In contrast to these doctrines, and utterly opposed to them, were the tenets of the Legalist school, which began to take shape late in the fourth century. Rejecting the beliefs and mores of the past, the Legalists sought by every means possible to strengthen the state and increase its military might. Old customs and moral codes were to be replaced by detailed laws that defined the duties of all groups in society and the penalties to be meted out if they failed to fulfill them. Agriculture and warfare were to be the prime concerns of the population, and the ruler was to have unlimited power to promote them and to see that other activities and doctrines that conflicted with these aims were suppressed.

Besides these major schools, there were others that devoted attention to questions of logic and semantics or to specialized subjects such as agriculture, military tactics, or geomancy and divination.

Evolving simultaneously with these various currents of thought was that represented by the text presented here, the school known as Taoism. Like many of the other schools, it looked back to an ideal age in the past, but one that predated the dawn of Chinese history and written culture, a kind of dream of Neolithic simplicity and innocence. Addressing the ruler, as did so many of the thinkers of the period, the Taoists counseled him to spurn both the earnest moral strivings of the Confucians and Mo-ists and the harsh and meddlesome measures of the Legalists and instead to adopt a policy of inaction, or laissez-faire.

Speaking to the ordinary men and women of these troublous times, the Taoists instructed them how to survive by crouching low and keeping out of the line of fire. What in particular sets the Taoists apart from the other schools of philosophy is the marked strain of mysticism and quietism that underlies so much of their thought, a strain that seems to reach far back into the roots of Chinese culture. It is this strain that in a Taoist text such as the *Tao Te Ching* engenders its most potent symbols: water, darkness, the valley, the female, the babe.

The *Tao Te Ching*

Early Taoism is known to us through two famous works, the *Chuang-tzu* and the *Lao-tzu* or *Tao Te Ching*, both of uncertain date but originating probably in the fourth or third century B.C.E. The *Chuang-tzu*, in thirty-three sections, is made up of writings attributed to the philosopher Chuang Chou (flourished fourth century). The *Tao Te Ching*, in two parts and eighty-one short sections, has traditionally been attributed to a figure known as Lao-tzu, or the "Old Master."

The earliest biographical account of Lao-tzu is that found in chapter 63 of the *Shih chi*, or *Records of the Historian*, a voluminous work on Chinese history written around 100 B.C.E. by Ssu-ma Ch'ien. According to that brief notice, Lao-tzu's surname was Li, his personal names were Erh and Tan, and he was a native of Ch'u, a large state situated in the lower Yangtze valley. He served as historian in

charge of the archives of the Chou court, which means he must have resided at the Chou capital in Lo-yang.

The account gives no dates for his lifetime but states that when Confucius one time visited the Chou capital, he questioned Lao-tzu concerning matters of ritual. From this it has been assumed that Lao-tzu was a contemporary of Confucius.

After describing the meeting between the two philosophers, the biography goes on to say that Lao-tzu, "viewing the decline of the Chou royal house, eventually quit the capital and journeyed to the Pass," presumably the Han-ku Pass, far west of Lo-yang. There the Keeper of the Pass, surmising that the old man was about to withdraw from the world, asked if he would write a book for him before doing so. "Lao-tzu thereupon wrote a work in two parts, expounding the meaning of *tao* and *te* in some five thousand characters, and then departed." "What became of him afterward," the historian adds, "no one knows."

Scholars both in China and elsewhere have long eyed this account with grave suspicion, and many now regard Lao-tzu as a purely legendary figure. Yet the story of how the book came to be written, apocryphal though it may be, seems to hover about its pages even today, and the scene of the old philosopher taking leave of the Keeper of the Pass before setting off into the unknown has never ceased to be a favorite subject with artists of China and the other countries within the Chinese cultural sphere.

The title *Tao Te Ching*, or *Classic of Tao and Te*, derives, then, from the fact that, as indicated in Ssu-ma Ch'ien's

account, these two concepts constitute the core of the philosophy expounded in the work. *Tao* (pronounced like the "dow" in "down"), the term from which the school of Taoism takes its name, means literally a "way" or "path" and is used by other schools of philosophy to refer to a particular calling or mode of conduct. But in Taoist writings it has a far more comprehesive meaning, referring rather to a metaphysical first principle that embraces and underlies all being, a vast Oneness that precedes and in some mysterious manner generates the endlessly diverse forms of the world. Ultimately, as the *Tao Te Ching* stresses, *tao* lies beyond the power of language to describe, though the text employs a number of highly suggestive terms and similes to allude to it, kennings for the ineffable, as it were, that serve to suggest at least something of its nature and immensity. For, unknowable as the *tao* may be in essence, one must somehow learn to sense its presence and movement in order to bring one's own life and movements into harmony with it. The aim of the text, then, is to impart to the reader, though hints, symbols, and paradoxical utterances, such an intuitive grasp of the *tao* and the vital ability to move with it rather than counter to it.

The second key term, *te* (pronounced like the "du" in "dud"), is likewise common in early Chinese historical and philosophical literature and denotes a moral power or virtue characteristic of a person who follows a correct course of conduct. It is pronounced the same as and is probably cognate with another word meaning "to get," and in Taoism this aspect of meaning is stressed over the purely

moral one; that is, *te* is the virtue or power that one acquires through being in accord with the *tao,* what one "gets" from the *tao.*

It is hoped that the reader will be able to gain a deeper and fuller understanding of these key concepts and their implications from a reading of the text itself. But one should not approach the *Tao Te Ching* expecting to find any systematic or logical exposition of ideas or careful definition of terms, such as one might encounter in a work of Greek philosophy or for that matter in some of the works of other schools of Chinese philosophy. Such is not the Taoist manner of imparting wisdom.

Nearly all early Chinese thinkers rely heavily on anecdotes from history, or what they claim to be history, to illustrate their ideas. Chuang Chou, the other major Taoist philosopher mentioned earlier, is no exception, though his anecdotes make only slight pretense at being historical and in fact include such personages as talking trees, birds, and animals. The *Tao Te Ching,* on the other hand, is all but unique in early Chinese literature in that it does not contain a single reference to history or personal names of any kind. The speaker and those to and about whom he or she speaks are all equally anonymous, and the pronouncements of the text dwell in a kind of void, like so many timeless axioms, which is what they have often been compared to.

Classical Chinese, the language of the texts I have been discussing, is highly terse and compressed in expression. This verbal economy, along with the intrinsic aesthetic appeal of the written characters, make Chinese an

ideal medium for mottoes and slogans. Down through the centuries the Chinese have in fact shown an abiding fondness for pithy inscriptions, in ancient times incising them on bronze vessels or stones, later painting them on plaques and gateways, and most recently displaying them in the form of wall posters.

The "Great Learning," a chapter of the Confucian *Book of Rites*, relates that King T'ang, the sage founder of the Shang dynasty, had an inscription on his bathtub that, in three tidy phrases of three characters each, read: "If daily renewal, daily daily renewal, again daily renewal!" So far as meaning goes, this seems to say little more than "Take a bath every day and you'll feel like a new person." But because of the repetitions and extreme terseness, it achieves a force and resonance far transcending the mere semantic content.

This same aura of depth and urgency pervades the pronouncements of the *Tao Te Ching*. Devoid of context, with all superfluous syntax and connectives lopped away, they stand like so many stone inscriptions, peering out at us from a mysterious and shadowy place. As the translators point out, it is this numinous and evasive quality in the text that accounts for its perennial appeal. The words do not readily yield up their message but seem to recede farther into obscurity the more assiduously one struggles with them, which is no doubt why so many exegetes and translators have tackled them over the centuries, determined to wrest them into meaning.

Of course these texts of the late Chou philosophers, the *Tao Te Ching* among them, do not exist in isolation but

speak back and forth to one another, refuting each other's arguments, borrowing terminology from one another and defining it in new ways. Many passages in the *Tao Te Ching* are clearly meant to refer to or confute the teachings of the Confucians or the Legalists, and its language utilizes the same literary devices of repetition, parallelism, and occasional end rhyme that the other philosophers employ to ornament their style and lend it elegance. But the *Tao Te Ching* lacks a specific speaker or context and because it relies not on logical exposition but on sheer power of language in expounding its ideas, it comes closer to pure poetry than do any of the other philosophical texts. It is this poetic force and beauty of the text that the translators, as they explain in their preface, have been most concerned to bring across in their translation. It seems to me they have succeeded brilliantly.

TAO TE CHING

Tao

I

Tao called Tao is not Tao.

Names can name no lasting name.

Nameless: the origin of heaven and earth.
Naming: the mother of ten thousand things.

Empty of desire, perceive mystery.
Filled with desire, perceive manifestations.

These have the same source, but different names.
　　　Call them both deep—
　　　　　Deep and again deep:

The gateway to all mystery.

道可道非常道

Tao called Tao is not Tao
Tao k'o tao fei ch'ang tao

2

Recognize beauty and ugliness is born.
Recognize good and evil is born.

Is and Isn't produce each other.

> Hard depends on easy,
> Long is tested by short,
> High is determined by low,
> Sound is harmonized by voice,
> After is followed by before.

Therefore the Sage is devoted to non-action,
Moves without teaching,
Creates ten thousand things without instruction,
Lives but does not own,
Acts but does not presume,
Accomplishes without taking credit.

When no credit is taken,
Accomplishment endures.

Is and Isn't produce each other
Ku yu wu hsiang sheng

故
有
無
相
生

3

Don't glorify heroes,
And people will not contend.
Don't treasure rare objects,
And no one will steal.
Don't display what people desire,
And their hearts will not be disturbed.

Therefore,
The Sage rules
  By emptying hearts and filling bellies,
  By weakening ambitions and strengthening bones;
Leads people
  Away from knowing and wanting:
Deters those who know too much
  From going too far:
Practices non-action
  And the natural order is not disrupted.

Don't glorify heroes
Pu shang hsien

不
尚
賢

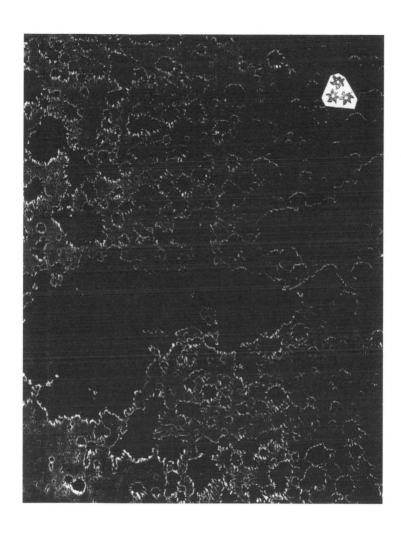

4

Tao is empty—
    Its use never exhausted.
Bottomless—
    The origin of all things.

It blunts sharp edges,
    Unties knots,
    Softens glare,
    Becomes one with the dusty world.

Deeply subsistent—
I don't know whose child it is.

It is older than the Ancestor.

Tao is empty   道
Tao ch'ung   冲

Not Kind

5

Heaven and Earth are not kind:
The ten thousand things are straw dogs to them.

Sages are not kind:
People are straw dogs to them.

Yet Heaven and Earth
And all the space between
Are like a bellows:
Empty but inexhaustible,
Always producing more.

Longwinded speech is exhausting.
       Better to stay centered.

Heaven and Earth are not kind

T'ien ti pu jen

天
地
不
仁

6

The Valley Spirit never dies.
It is called the Mysterious Female.

The entrance to the Mysterious Female
Is called the root of Heaven and Earth,

Endless flow
Of inexhaustible energy.

It is called the Mysterious Female
Shih wei hsüan p'in 是謂玄牝

7

Heaven is long, Earth enduring.

Long and enduring
Because they do not exist for themsel..

Therefore the Sage
     Steps back, but is always in front,
     Stays outside, but is always within.

No self-interest?
Self is fulfilled.

Heaven is long, Earth enduring
T'ien ch'ang ti chiu

天長地久

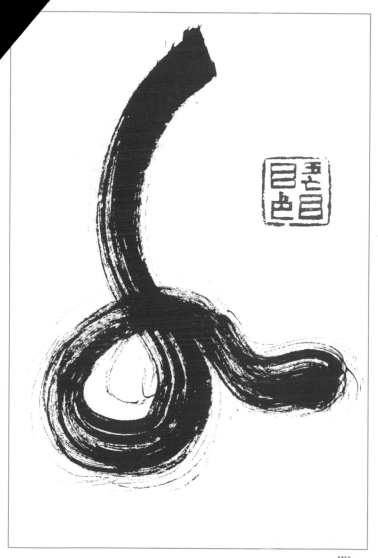

Water

8

Best to be like water,
Which benefits the ten thousand things
And does not contend.
It pools where humans disdain to dwell,
Close to the Tao.

> Live in a good place.
> Keep your mind deep.
> Treat others well.
> Stand by your word.
> Keep good order.
> Do the right thing.
> Work when it's time.

> Only do not contend,
And you will not go wrong.

Best to be like water

Shang shan jo shui

上善若水

9

Hold and fill it—
Not as good as stopping in time.

Measure and pound it—
It will not long survive.

When gold and jade fill the hall,
They cannot be guarded.

Riches and pride
Bequeath error.

Withdrawing when work is done:
      Heaven's Tao.

Heaven's Tao 天
T'ien chih tao 之
道

Can you balance your life force
And embrace the One
Without separation?

Can you control your breath
Gently
Like a baby?

Can you clarify
Your dark vision
Without blemish?

Can you love people
And govern the country
Without knowledge?

Can you open and close
The gate of heaven
Without clinging to earth?

Can you brighten
The four directions
Without action?

> Give birth and cultivate.
> Give birth and do not possess.
> Act without dependence.
> Excel but do not rule.
> This is called dark Te.

This is called dark Te

Shih wei hsüan te

是謂玄德

One

Thirty spokes join one hub.
The wheel's use comes from emptiness.

Clay is fired to make a pot.
The pot's use comes from emptiness.

Windows and doors are cut to make a room.
The room's use comes from emptiness.

Therefore,
> Having leads to profit,
> Not having leads to use.

Not having leads to use

Wu chih i wei yung

無之以爲用

Five colors darken the eyes.
Five tones deaden the ears.
Five tastes jade the palate.
Hunting and racing madden the heart.
Exotic goods ensnarl human lives.

Therefore the Sage
    Takes care of the belly, not the eye,
    Chooses one, rejects the other.

Five colors darken the eyes

Wu se ling jen mu mang

五色令人目盲

13

Favor and disgrace are like fear.
Honor and distress are like the self.

What does this mean?

Favor debases us.
Afraid when we get it,
Afraid when we lose it.

The self embodies distress.
     No self,
     No distress.

Respect the world as your self:
     The world can be your lodging.
Love the world as your self:
     The world can be your trust.

Favor and disgrace are like fear

Ch'ung ju jo ching

寵辱若驚

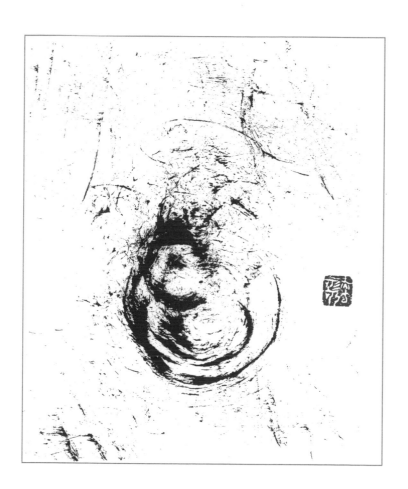

14

Searching but not seeing, we call it dim.
Listening but not hearing, we call it faint.
Groping but not touching, we call it subtle.

These three cannot be fully grasped.
Therefore they become one.

Rising it is not bright; setting it is not dark.
It moves all things back to where there is nothing.

Meeting it there is no front,
Following it there is no back.

Live in the ancient Tao,
Master the existing present,
Understand the source of all things.
This is called the record of Tao.

This is called the record of Tao

Shih wei tao chi

是謂道紀

The ancients who followed Tao:
Dark, wondrous, profound, penetrating,
Deep beyond knowing.

Because they cannot be known,
They can only be described.

Cautious,
    Like crossing a winter stream.
Hesitant,
    Like respecting one's neighbors.
Polite,
    Like a guest.
Yielding,
    Like ice about to melt.
Blank,
    Like uncarved wood.
Open,
    Like a valley.
Mixing freely,
    Like muddy water.

Dark, wondrous, profound, penetrating

Wei, miao, hsüan, t'ung

微
妙
玄
通

Calm the muddy water,
　　　It becomes clear.
Move the inert,
　　　It comes to life.

Those who sustain Tao
　　　Do not wish to be full.

Because they do not wish to be full
　　　They can fade away
　　　　　Without further effort.

Attain complete emptiness,
Hold fast to stillness.

The ten thousand things stir about;
I only watch for their going back.

Things grow and grow,
But each goes back to its root.
Going back to the root is stillness.
This means returning to what is.
Returning to what is
Means going back to the ordinary.

Understanding the ordinary:
    Enlightenment.

Not understanding the ordinary:
    Blindness creates evil.

Understanding the ordinary:
    Mind opens.

Attain complete emptiness
Chih hsü chi

致
虛
極

Mind opening leads to compassion,
Compassion to nobility,
Nobility to heavenliness,
Heavenliness to Tao.

> Tao endures.
> Your body dies.

There is no danger.

17

Great rising and falling—
　　　　People only know it exists.
Next they see and praise.
Soon they fear.
Finally they despise.

Without fundamental trust
There is no trust at all.

Be careful in valuing words.
When the work is done,
　　　　Everyone says
We just acted naturally.

Great rising and falling 太上下
T'ai shang hsia

Great Tao rejected:
>   Benevolence and righteousness appear.

Learning and knowledge professed:
>   Great hypocrites spring up.

Family relations forgotten:
>   Filial piety and affection arise.

The nation disordered:
>   Patriots come forth.

Great Tao rejected
Ta tao fei

大
道
廢

Banish learning, discard knowledge:
People will gain a hundredfold.

Banish benevolence, discard righteousness:
People will return to duty and compassion.

Banish skill, discard profit:
There will be no more thieves.

These three statements are not enough.
One more step is necessary:

Look at plain silk; hold uncarved wood.
The self dwindles; desires fade.

Banish learning, discard knowledge
Chüeh sheng ch'i chih

絕聖棄智

Banish learning, no more grief.
Between Yes and No
How much difference?
Between good and evil
How much difference?
What others fear I must fear—
How pointless!

People are wreathed in smiles
As if at a carnival banquet.
I alone am passive, giving no sign,
Like an infant who has not yet smiled.
Forlorn, as if I had no home.

Others have enough and more,
I alone am left out.
I have the mind of a fool,
Confused, confused.

Others are bright and intelligent,
I alone am dull, dull,
Drifting on the ocean,
Blown about endlessly.

Others have plans,
I alone am wayward and stubborn,
I alone am different from others,
Like a baby in the womb.

Confused, confused
T'un t'un hsi

沌
沌
兮

Te

Great Te appears
Flowing from Tao.

Tao in action—
Only vague and intangible.

Intangible—vague—
Within it are images.

Vague—intangible—
Within it are entities.

Shadowy—obscure—
Within it there is life,

Life so real
That within it there is trust.

From the beginning its name is not lost
But reappears through multiple origins.

How do I know these origins? .

      Like this.

Shadowy—obscure—
Yao hsi ming hsi

窈
兮
冥
兮

Crooked

Crippled becomes whole,
Crooked becomes straight,
Hollow becomes full,
Worn becomes new,
Little becomes more,
Much becomes delusion.

Therefore Sages cling to the One
        And take care of this world;
Do not display themselves
        And therefore shine;
Do not assert themselves
        And therefore stand out;
Do not praise themselves
        And therefore succeed;
Are not complacent
        And therefore endure;
Do not control
        And therefore no one under heaven
                Can contend with them.

The old saying
Crippled becomes whole
Is not empty words.

It becomes whole and returns.

Crippled becomes whole

Ch'ü tse ch'üan

23

Spare words: nature's way.

Violent winds do not blow all morning.
Sudden rain cannot pour all day.
What causes these things?
Heaven and Earth.

If Heaven and Earth do not blow and pour for long,
How much less should humans?

Therefore in following Tao:
> Those on the way become the way,
> Those who gain become the gain,
> Those who lose become the loss.

All within Tao:
> The wayfarer, welcome upon the way,
> Those who gain, welcome within gain,
> Those who lose, welcome within loss.

Without trust in this
There is no trust at all.

Spare words: nature's way

Hsi yen tzu jan

希言自然

24

On tiptoe: no way to stand.
Clambering: no way to walk.
Self-display: no way to shine.
Self-assertion: no way to succeed.
Self-praise: no way to flourish.
Complacency: no way to endure.

According to Tao,
      Excessive food,
      Extraneous activity
      Inspire disgust.

Therefore, the follower of Tao
Moves on.

On tiptoe: no way to stand

Ch'i che pu li

企者不立

25

Something unformed and complete
Before heaven and earth were born,
Solitary and silent,
Stands alone and unchanging,
Pervading all things without limit.
It is like the mother of all under heaven,
But I don't know its name—
> Better call it Tao.
> Better call it great.

Great means passing on.
Passing on means going far.
Going far means returning.

Therefore,
> Tao is great,
> And heaven,
> And earth,
> And humans.

Four great things in the world.
Aren't humans one of them?

Humans follow earth
Earth follows heaven
Heaven follows Tao.

Tao follows its own nature.

Tao follows its own nature
Tao fa tzu jan

道法自然

Gravity is the root of lightness,
Stillness is the master of passion.

The Sage travels all day
But does not leave the baggage-cart;
When surrounded by magnificent scenery
Remains calm and still.

When a lord of ten thousand chariots
Behaves lightly in this world,
Lightness loses its root,
Passion loses its master.

Gravity is the root of lightness

Chung wei ch'ing ken

重爲輕根

Good travellers leave no tracks.
Good words leave no trace.
Good counting needs no markers.

Good doors have no bolts
  Yet cannot be forced.
Good knots have no rope
  But cannot be untied.

In this way the Sage
  Always helps people
  And rejects none,
  Always helps all beings,
  And rejects none.
This is called practicing brightness.

Therefore the good person
  Is the bad person's teacher,
And the bad person
  Is the good person's resource.

  Not to value the teacher,
  Not to love the resource,
Causes great confusion even for the intelligent.

This is called the vital secret.

This is called the vital secret
Shih wei yao miao

是謂要妙

28

Know the male, maintain the female,
Become the channel of the world.

Become the channel of the world,
And Te will endure.

Return to infancy.

Know the white, sustain the black,
Become the pattern of the world.

Become the pattern of the world,
And Te will not falter.

Return to the uncarved block.

Know honor, sustain disgrace,
Become the valley of the world,
And Te will prevail.

Return to simplicity.

Simplicity divided becomes utensils
That are used by the Sage as high official.
But great governing does not carve up.

知其雄　守其雌

Know the male, maintain the female
Chih ch'i hsiung, shou ch'i tz'u

29

Trying to control the world?
I see you won't succeed.

The world is a spiritual vessel
And cannot be controlled.

Those who control, fail.
Those who grasp, lose.

Some go forth, some are led,
Some weep, some blow flutes,
Some become strong, some superfluous,
Some oppress, some are destroyed.

Therefore the Sage
      Casts off extremes,
      Casts off excess,
      Casts off extravagance.

The world is a spiritual vessel

T'ien hsia shen ch'i

天下神器

30

Use Tao to help rule people.

This world has no need for weapons,
Which soon turn on themselves.
Where armies camp, nettles grow;
After each war, years of famine.

The most fruitful outcome
Does not depend on force,
But succeeds without arrogance
     Without hostility
     Without pride
     Without resistance
     Without violence.

If these things prosper and grow old,
This is called not-Tao.
Not-Tao soon ends.

Not-Tao soon ends

Pu tao tsao i

Fine weapons are ill-omened tools.
  They are hated.
Therefore the old Taoist ignores them.

At home, honor the left.
In war, honor the right.

Weapons are ill-omened tools,
Not proper instruments.
When their use can't be avoided,
Calm restraint is best.

Don't think they are beautiful.
Those who think they are beautiful
Rejoice in killing people.

Those who rejoice in killing people
Cannot achieve their purpose in this world.

Good omens honor the left.
Bad omens honor the right.
The lieutenant on the left,
The general on the right,
As in funeral ceremonies.

When many people are killed
We feel sorrow and grief.

A great victory
Is a funeral ceremony.

Weapons are ill-omened tools
Ping che pu hsiang chih ch'i

兵者不祥之器

Tao

32

Tao endures without a name.
Though simple and slight,
No one under heaven can master it.

If kings and lords could possess it,
All beings would become their guests.
Heaven and earth together
Would drip sweet dew
Equally on all people
Without regulation.

Begin to make order, and names arise.
Names lead to more names—
And to knowing when to stop.

Know when to stop:
Avoid danger.

Tao's presence in this world
Is like valley streams
Flowing into rivers and seas.

Tao endures without a name

Tao ch'ang wu ming

道
常
無
名

Knowing others is intelligent.
Knowing yourself is enlightened.

Conquering others takes force.
Conquering yourself is true strength.

Knowing what is enough is wealth.
Forging ahead shows inner resolve.

Hold your ground and you will last long.
Die without perishing and your life will endure.

Knowing yourself is enlightened

Tzu chih che ming

自
知
者
明

34

Great Tao overflows
To the left.   To the right.

All beings owe their life to it
And do not depart from it.
It acts without a name.
It clothes and nourishes all beings
But does not become their master.

Enduring without desire,
It may be called slight.
All beings return to it,
But it does not become their master.

It may be called immense.
By not making itself great,
It can do great things.

Great Tao overflows

Ta tao fan hsi

大道氾兮

35

Hold the great elephant
And the world moves.
Moves without danger
In safety and peace.

Music and sweets
Make passing guests pause,
But the Tao emerges
Flavorless and bland.

Look—
      You won't see it.
Listen—
      You won't hear it.
Use it—
      You will never use it up.

Hold the great elephant

Chih ta hsiang　執大象

36

To collect, first scatter.
To weaken, first strengthen.
To abolish, first establish.
To conclude, first initiate.

This is called subtle illumination.

Soft and weak overcome stiff and strong.
Fish cannot escape the deep pool.
A country's sharpest weapons
Cannot be displayed.

This is called subtle illumination

Shih wei wei ming

是謂微明

No, Nothing

37

Tao endures without a name,
Yet nothing is left undone.
If kings and lords could possess it,
All beings would transform themselves.

Transformed, they desire to create;
I quiet them through nameless simplicity.
Then there is no desire.

No desire is serenity,
And the world settles of itself.

No desire is serenity
Pu yü i ching

38

High Te? No Te!
      That's what Te is.
Low Te doesn't lack Te;
      That's what Te is not.

Those highest in Te take no action
      And don't need to act.
Those lowest in Te take action
      And do need to act.

Those highest in benevolence take action
      But don't need to act.
Those highest in righteousness take action
      And do need to act.
Those highest in propriety take action
      And if people don't reciprocate
      Roll up their sleeves and throw them out.

Therefore,
Lose Tao
      And Te follows.
Lose Te
      And benevolence follows.
Lose benevolence
      And righteousness follows.
Lose righteousness
      And propriety follows.

High Te? No Te!

Shang te pu te

上德不德

Propriety dilutes loyalty and sincerity:
      Confusion begins.
Foreknowledge glorifies the Tao:
      Stupidity sets in.

And so the ideal person dwells
      In substance, not dilution;
      In reality, not glory;
Accepts one, rejects the other.

39

Of old, these attained the One:

> Heaven attaining the One
> > Became clear.
> Earth attaining the One
> > Became stable.
> Spirits attaining the One
> > Became sacred.
> Valleys attaining the One
> > Became bountiful.
> Myriad beings attaining the One
> > Became fertile.
> Lords and kings attaining the One
> > Purified the world.

If Heaven were not clear
> It might split.
If Earth were not stable,
> It might erupt.
If spirits were not sacred
> They might fade.
If valleys were not bountiful
> They might wither.
If myriad beings were not fertile,
> They might perish.
If rulers and lords were not noble,
> They might stumble.

Therefore,

      Noble has humble as its root,

      High has low as its foundation.

Rulers and lords call themselves

      Poor lonely orphans.

Isn't this using humility as a root?

They use many carriages

      But have no carriage;

They do not desire to glisten like jade

      But drop, drop like a stone.

But drop, drop like a stone

Lo lo ju shih

落落如石

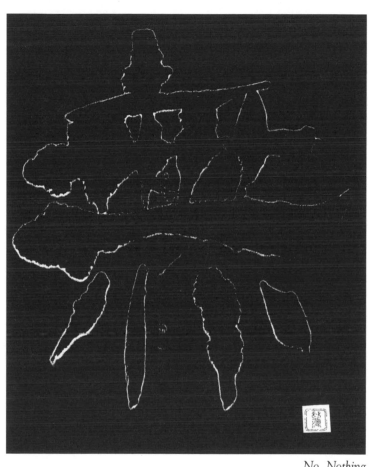

No, Nothing

40

Reversal is Tao's movement.

Yielding is Tao's practice.

All things originate from being.

Being originates from non-being.

Being originates from non-being
Yu sheng yü wu.

有
生
於
無

Laugh, Smile

The great scholar hearing the Tao
    Tries to practice it.
The middling scholar hearing the Tao
    Sometimes has it, sometimes not.
The lesser scholar hearing the Tao
    Has a good laugh.
Without that laughter
    It wouldn't be Tao.

    Therefore, these sayings:

The bright road seems dark,
The road forward seems to retreat,
The level road seems rough.

Great Te seems hollow.
Great purity seems sullied.
Pervasive Te seems deficient.
Established Te seems furtive.
Simple truths seem to change.

The great square has no corners.
The great vessel is finished late.
The great sound is scarcely voiced.
The great image has no form.

Tao hides, no name.

Yet Tao alone gets things done.

Tao hides, no name
Tao yin wu ming

道隱無名

42

Tao engenders One,
One engenders Two,
Two engenders Three,
Three engenders the ten thousand things.

The ten thousand things carry shade
And embrace sunlight.
      Shade and sunlight, yin and yang,
Breath blending into harmony.

Humans hate
To be alone, poor, and hungry.
Yet kings and princes
Use these words as titles.
      We gain by losing,
      Lose by gaining.

What others teach, I also teach:
A violent man does not die a natural death.
This is the basis of my teaching.

Tao engenders One

Tao sheng i

道
生
一

43

The softest thing in the world
Rides roughshod over the strongest.

No-thing enters no-space.

This teaches me the benefit of no-action.

Teaching without words,
Benefit without action—

Few in this world can attain this.

No-thing enters no-space
Wu yu ju wu chien

無有入無間

44

Name or body: which is closer?
Body or possessions: which means more?
Gain or loss: which one hurts?

Extreme love exacts a great price.
Many possessions entail heavy loss.

Know what is enough—
    Abuse nothing.
Know when to stop—
    Harm nothing.

This is how to last a long time.

Name or body: which is closer?

Ming yü shen shu ch'in

名與身孰親

45

Great accomplishment seems unfinished
    But its use is continuous.

Great fullness seems empty
    But in use is inexhaustible.

Great straightness seems bent,
Great skill seems clumsy,
Great eloquence seems mute.

Exertion overcomes cold.
Calm overcomes heat.

Pure calm is the norm under heaven.

Pure calm is the norm under heaven
Ch'ing ching wei t'ien hsia cheng

清靜爲天下正

46

With Tao under heaven
>Stray horses fertilize the fields.
Without Tao under heaven
>Warhorses are bred at the frontier.

There is no greater calamity
>Than not knowing what is enough.
There is no greater fault
>Than desire for success.

>Therefore,
Knowing that enough is enough
>Is always
>>Enough.

With Tao under heaven

T'ien hsia yu tao

天
下
有
道

See

47

Without going out the door,
    Know the world.
Without peeping through the window,
    See heaven's Tao.

The further you travel,
    The less you know.   .

This is why the Sage
    Knows without budging,
    Identifies without looking,
    Does without trying.

See heaven's Tao

Chien t'ien tao

見天道

Pursue knowledge, gain daily.
Pursue Tao, lose daily.
Lose and again lose,
Arrive at non-doing.

Non-doing—and nothing not done.

Take the entire world as nothing.
Make the least effort
And the world escapes you.

Non-doing—and nothing not done

Wu wei erh wu pu wei

無爲而無不爲

49

The Sage has no set heart.

> Ordinary people's hearts
> Become the Sage's heart.

People who are good
> I treat well.
People who are not good
> I also treat well:
>> Te as goodness.

Trustworthy people
> I trust.
Untrustworthy people
> I also trust:
>> Te as trust.

Sages create harmony under heaven
> Blending their hearts with the world.
Ordinary people fix their eyes and ears on them,
> But Sages become the world's children.

Te as goodness　　德善
Te shan

Te as trust　　德信
Te hsin

50

Emerge into life, enter death.

Life is only the thirteen body parts,
Death is only the thirteen body parts.

Human life, moving towards death,
Is the same thirteen.

Why is this?

Because life gives life to substance.

You have heard of people
      Good at holding on to life.
Walking overland they don't avoid
      Rhinos and tigers.
In battle they don't arm themselves.
The rhino's horn finds nothing to gore,
The tiger's claws find nothing to flay,
Weapons find nothing to pierce.

Why is this?

They have no mortal spot.

Emerge into life, enter death

Ch'u sheng ju szu

出
生
入
死

Tao bears them
Te nurses them
Events form them
Energy completes them.

Therefore the ten thousand beings
Honor Tao and respect Te.

Tao is honored
Te is respected
Because they do not give orders
But endure in their own nature.

Therefore,
Tao bears them and Te nurses them,
      Rears them
      Raises them
      Shelters them
      Nurtures them
      Supports them
      Protects them

Bears them without owning them,
Helps them without coddling them,
Rears them without ruling them.

This is called original Te.

This is called original Te

Shih wei yüan te 是謂元德

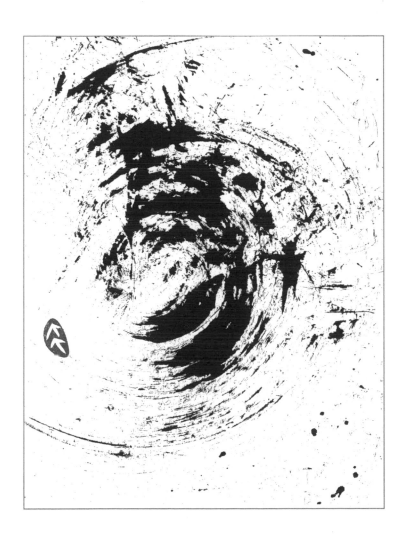

52

The world has a source: the world's mother.

Once you have the mother,
      You know the children.
Once you know the children,
      Return to the mother.

Your body dies.
There is no danger.

Block the passage,
Bolt the gate:
      No strain
Until your life ends.

Open the passage,
Take charge of things:
      No relief
Until your life ends.

Seeing the small is called brightness.
Maintaining gentleness is called strength.
Use this brightness to return to brightness.

Don't cling to your body's woes.
Then you can learn endurance.

Seeing the small is called brightness

Chien hsiao yüeh ming

見
小
曰
明

53

Having some knowledge
When walking the Great Tao
Only brings fear.

The Great Tao is very smooth,
But people like rough trails.

The government is divided,
Fields are overgrown,
Granaries are empty,
But the nobles' clothes are gorgeous,
Their belts show off swords,
And they are glutted with food and drink.
Personal wealth is excessive.

This is called thieves' endowment,
      But it is not Tao.

The Great Tao is very smooth

Ta tao shen i

大道甚夷

54

Well planted, not uprooted.
Well embraced, never lost.
　　　Descendants will continue
The ancestral rituals.

Maintain oneself:
　　　Te becomes real.
Maintain the family:
　　　Te becomes abundant.
Maintain the community:
　　　Te becomes extensive.
Maintain the country:
　　　Te becomes prolific.
Maintain the world:
　　　Te becomes omnipresent.

Therefore,
Through self contemplate self,
Through family contemplate family,
Through community contemplate community,
Through country contemplate country,
Through world contemplate world.

How do I know the world?

　　　Like this!

Like this　以
I tz'u　　此

55

Be filled with Te,
Like a baby:

Wasps, scorpions and vipers
Do not sting it.
Fierce tigers do not stalk it.
Birds of preys do not attack it.

Bones weak, muscles soft,
But its grasp is tight.

It does not yet know
Union of male and female,
But its sex is formed,
Its vital essence complete.

It can scream all day and not get hoarse.
Its harmony is complete.

Knowing harmony is called endurance.
Knowing endurance is called illumination.
Increasing life is called fortune.
Mind controlling energy is called power.

When beings prosper and grow old,
Call them not-Tao.
Not-Tao soon ends.

Not-Tao soon ends

Pu tao tsao i

不
道
早
已

Those who know don't talk.
Those who talk don't know.

Block the passage
Bolt the gate
Blunt the sharp
Untie the knot
Blend with the light
Become one with the dust—
This is called original unity.

It can't be embraced
It can't be escaped,
It can't be helped
It can't be harmed,
It can't be exalted
It can't be despised,

Therefore it is revered under Heaven.

知者不言

Those who know don't talk

Chih che pu yen

言者不知

Those who talk don't know

Yen che pu chih

57

Use the expected to govern the country,
Use surprise to wage war,
Use non-action to win the world.
How do I know?

Like this!

The more prohibitions and rules,
The poorer people become.
The sharper people's weapons,
The more they riot.
The more skilled their techniques,
The more grotesque their works.
The more elaborate the laws,
The more they commit crimes.

Therefore the Sage says:

I do nothing
And people transform themselves.
I enjoy serenity
And people govern themselves.
I cultivate emptiness
And people become prosperous.
I have no desires
And people simplify themselves.

I do nothing　我
Wo wu wei　無
　　　　　　爲

58

If government is muted and muffled
People are cool and refreshed.
If government investigates and intrudes,
People are worn down and hopeless.

Bad fortune rests upon good fortune.
Good luck hides within bad luck.

Who knows how it will end?

If there is no principle
Principle reverts to disorder,
Good reverts to calamity,
People's confusion hardens and lingers on.

   Therefore the Sage
Squares without cutting,
Corners without dividing,
Straightens without extending,
Shines without dazzling.

Shines without dazzling

Kuang erh pu yao

光而不燿

59

Governing people and serving heaven
    Is like living off the land.
Living sparingly and responding quickly
    Means accumulating Te.

There is nothing that cannot be overcome.
    There is no limit.

You can become the country
And the country's mother,
And nourish and extend it.

This is called deep roots, firm base.

This is the Tao of living long and seeing far.

是
謂
深
根
固
柢

This is called deep roots, firm base

Shih wei shen ken ku ti

60

Govern big countries
Like you cook little fish.

When Tao harmonizes the world,
Demons lose their power.

Not that demons lose their power,
But their power does not harm people.

Not that their power does not harm people,
But the Sage does not harm people.

If neither does harm,
Then Te flows and returns.

Then Te flows and returns

Ku te chiao kuei yen

故德交歸焉

61

A great nation flows down
To be the world's pool,
The female under heaven

    In stillness
The female constantly overcomes the male,
    In stillness
Takes the low place.

Therefore a great nation
    Lowers itself
    And wins over a small one.

A small nation
    Keeps itself low
    And wins over a great one.

Sometimes becoming low wins,
Sometimes staying low wins.

A great nation desires nothing more
Then to unite and protect people.
A small nation desires nothing more
Than to enter the service of people.

When both get what they wish
The great one should be low.

The female under heaven
T'ien hsia chih p'in

天下之牝

Tao is the mysterious center of all things,
>A treasure for those who are good,
>A refuge for those who are not.

Beautiful words can be traded,
Noble deeds can enhance reputations,
But if people lack them,
Why should they be rejected?

When the Son of Heaven is enthroned
And the Three Ministries installed,
Presenting jade discs
And four-horse chariots
Cannot compare to sitting still
And offering the Tao.

The ancients honored this Tao.
>Didn't they say:
Through it seekers find,
Through it the guilty escape?
This is why Tao is honored under Heaven.

道者萬物之奧

Tao is the mysterious center of all things

Tao che wan wu chih ao

No, Nothing

63

Act without acting
Serve without serving
Taste without tasting
     Big, little,
     Many, few—
Repay hatred with Te.

Map difficult through easy
Approach great through narrow.

The most difficult things in the world
Must be accomplished through the easiest.
The greatest things in the world
Must be accomplished through the smallest.

Therefore the Sage
Never attempts great things
And so accomplishes them.

Quick promises
     Mean little trust.
Everything easy
     Means great difficulty.
Thus for the Sage
     Everything is difficult,
And so in the end
     Nothing is difficult.

Act without acting
Wei wu wei

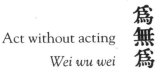

64

At rest is easy to hold.
Not yet impossible is easy to plan.
Brittle is easy to break.
Fine is easy to scatter.

Create before it exists.
Lead before it goes astray.

A tree too big to embrace
     Is born from a slender shoot.
A nine-storey tower
     Rises from a pile of earth.
A thousand-mile journey
     Begins with a single step.

Act and you ruin it.
Grasp and you lose it.
Therefore the Sage
     Does not act
     And so does not ruin
     Does not grasp
     And so does not lose.

Does not act   無爲
Wu wei

And so does not ruin   故無敗
Ku wu pai

People commonly ruin their work
     When they are near success.
Proceed at the end as at the beginning
     And your work won't be ruined.

Therefore the Sage
     Desires no desires
     Prizes no prizes
     Studies no studies
       And returns
     To what others pass by.

The Sage
     Helps all beings find their nature,
     But does not presume to act.

Te

65

Taoist rulers of old
>Did not enlighten people
But left them dull.

People are difficult to govern
Because they are very clever.

Therefore,
Ruling through cleverness
>Leads to rebellion.
Not ruling through cleverness
>Brings good fortune.
Know these two things
>And understand the enduring pattern.

Understand the enduring pattern:
>This is called original Te.

Original Te goes deep and far.
>All things reverse
>>Return
>And reach the great headwaters.

This is called original Te

Shih wei yüan te

是
謂
元
德

Sea, Ocean

66

Rivers and seas
  Can rule the hundred valleys.
Because they are good at lying low
They are lords of the valleys.

Therefore those who would be above
Must speak as if they are below.
Those who would lead
Must speak as if they are behind.

In this way the Sage dwells above
And the people are not burdened.
Dwells in front
And they are not hindered.

Therefore the whole world
Is delighted and unwearied.

Since the Sage does not contend
No one can contend with the Sage.

Rivers and seas   江
Chiang hai   海

Everyone under heaven calls my Tao great,
And unlike anything else.

It is great only because
It is unlike anything else.
If it were like anything else
It would stretch and become thin.

I have three treasures
To maintain and conserve:
The first is compassion.
The second is frugality.
The third is not presuming
To be first under heaven.

Compassion leads to courage.
Frugality allows generosity.
Not presuming to be first
Creates a lasting instrument.

Nowadays,
People reject compassion
But want to be brave,
Reject frugality
But want to be generous,
Reject humility
And want to come first.

This is death.

Everyone under heaven calls my Tao great

T'ien hsia chieh wei wo tao ta

天下皆謂我道大

Compassion:

>Attack with it and win.
>Defend with it and stand firm.

Heaven aids and protects

>Through compassion.

Not Contending

The accomplished person is not aggressive.
The good soldier is not hot-tempered.
The best conqueror does not engage the enemy.
The most effective leader takes the lowest place.

This is called the Te of not contending.
This is called the power of the leader.
This is called matching Heaven's ancient ideal.

This is called the Te of not contending

Shih wei pu cheng chih te

是謂不爭之德

69

There is a saying in the army:
I do not presume to be the master,
    But become the guest.
I do not dare advance an inch,
    But retreat a foot.

This is called moving without moving,
Rolling up sleeves without baring your arms,
Repelling without opposing,
Wielding without a weapon.

There is no disaster greater than
Contempt for the enemy.
    Contempt for the enemy—
What a treasure is lost!

Therefore,
When the fighting gets hot,
Those who grieve will conquer.

This is called moving without moving

Shih wei hsing wu hsing

是謂行無行

My words are very easy to understand,
Very easy to practice.

No one under heaven can understand them,
No one can practice them.

Words have ancestors,
Deeds have masters.
If people don't understand this,
They don't understand me.

Few understand me,
And this is my value.

Therefore the Sage wears rough clothing
And carries jade inside.

My words are very easy to understand
Wu yen shen i chih　吾言甚易知

Know not-knowing: supreme.

Not know knowing: faulty.

Only faulting faults is faultless.
The Sage is faultless
By faulting faults,
And so is without fault.

Know not-knowing: supreme
Chih pu chih shang

知
不
知
上

Not know knowing: faulty
Pu chih chih ping

不
知
知
病

When people are not in awe of power,
Power becomes great.

Do not intrude into their homes,
Do not make their lives weary.
        If you do not weary them,
They will not become weary of you.

Therefore the Sage
        Has self-knowledge without self-display,
        Self-love without personal pride.
Rejects one, accepts the other.

Power becomes great

Tse ta wei chih

則大威至

Tao

73

Courage to dare kills,
Courage not to dare saves.

One brings profit, one brings harm.

Heaven hates what it hates—
        Who knows why?
Even the Sage finds it difficult.

Heaven's Tao does not contend
        But prevails,
Does not speak
        But responds
Is not summoned
        But arrives,
Is utterly still
        But plans all actions.

Heaven's net is wide, wide,
Loose—
        But nothing slips through.

Heaven's Tao does not contend
T'ien chih tao pu cheng

天之道不爭

74

If people do not fear death,
How can you threaten them with death?
But if people with a normal fear of death
Are about to do something vicious,
And I could seize and execute them,
Who would dare?

There is always an official executioner.
Trying to take the executioner's place
Is like trying to replace a master woodworker—
Few would not slice their own hands.

Who would dare?

Shu kan 執敢

75

People are hungry.

> When rulers tax grain
> People are hungry.

People are rebellious.

> When rulers are active
> People are rebellious.

People ignore death.

> When searching only for life's bounty
> People ignore death.

Only those who don't strive after life
Truly respect life.

People are hungry
Min chih chi　民之饑

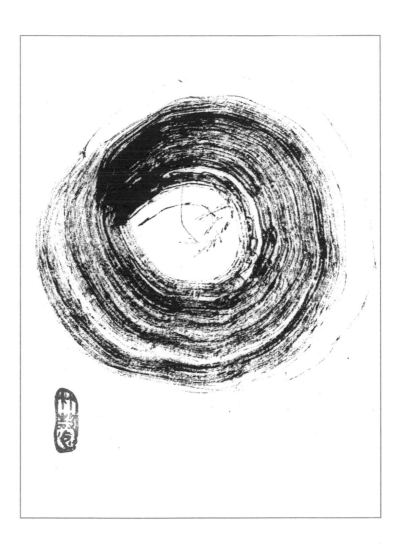

76

Humans are born soft and weak.
They die stiff and strong.
The ten thousand plants and trees
Are born soft and tender
And die withered and sere.

The stiff and strong
    Are Death's companions
The soft and weak
    Are Life's companions.

Therefore,
    The strongest armies do not conquer,
    The greatest trees are cut down.

    The strong and great sink down.
    The soft and weak rise up.

The soft and weak rise up

Jou jo ch'u shang

柔弱處上

Heaven's Tao
Is a stretched bow,
Pulling down the top,
Pulling up the bottom.
If it's too much, cut.
If it's not enough,
Add on to it:
Heaven's
Tao.

The Human Route
Is not like this,
Depriving the poor,
Offering to the rich.

Who has a surplus
And still offers it to the world?
Only those with Tao.

Therefore the Sage
Acts and expects nothing,
Accomplishes and does not linger,
Has no desire to seem worthy.

Heaven's Tao
T'ien chih tao

天
之
道

Nothing in the world is soft and weak as water.
But when attacking the hard and strong
Nothing can conquer so easily.

Weak overcomes strong,
Soft overcomes hard.

> Everyone knows this,
> No one attains it.

Therefore the Sage says:
> Accept a country's filth
> And become master of its sacred soil.
> Accept a country's ill fortune
> And become kind under heaven.

True words resemble their opposites.

True words resemble their opposites
Cheng yen jo fan

正言若反

Appease great hatred
And hatred will remain.

How can this be good?

Therefore the Sage
Holds the tally
But does not judge people.
Those who have Te
Control the tally.
Those who lack Te
Collect their due.

Heaven's Tao has no favorites
But endures in good people.

Heaven's Tao has no favorites
T'ien tao wu ch'in

天
道
無
親

Small country, few people—
    Hundreds of devices,
    But none are used.

People ponder on death
    And don't travel far.
They have carriages and boats,
    But no one goes on board;
Weapons and armor,
    But no one brandishes them.
They use knotted cords for counting.

    Sweet their food,
    Beautiful their clothes,
    Peaceful their homes,
    Delightful their customs.

Neighboring countries are so close
    You can hear their chickens and dogs.
But people grow old and die
    Without needing to come and go.

Small country, few people—
Hsiao kuo kua min

Sincere words are not pretty.
Pretty words are not sincere.

Good people do not quarrel.
Quarrelsome people are not good.
The wise are not learned.
The learned are not wise.

The Sage is not acquisitive—
　　　　Has enough
By doing for others,
　　　　Has even more
By giving to others.

Heaven's Tao
　　　　Benefits and does not harm.
The Sage's Tao
　　　　Acts and does not contend.

Sincere words are not pretty

Hsin yen pu mei

信言不美

Pretty words are not sincere

Mei yen pu hsin

美言不信

GLOSSARY OF CHINESE WORDS

The numbers below refer to the sections where the Chinese words can be found.

ao	奥	Center, mysterious, 62
ch'ang	常	Common, enduring, lasting, 1, 32
ch'ang	長	Long, excelling, 7
che	者	Person, 24, 31, 33, 56, 62
cheng	正	Correct, norm, 45, 78
cheng	爭	Contend, 68, 73
chi	紀	Record, history, 14
chi	極	Extreme, most, 16
chi	饑	Hungry, starve, 75
ch'i	棄	Discard, throw away, 19
ch'i	企	On tiptoe, anxious, 24
ch'i	其	This, that, 28
ch'i	器	Vessel, utensil, 29, 31

chiang　江　River, 66

chiao　交　Mingle, mix, flow, 60

chieh　皆　All, everyone, 67

chien　間　Space, 43
chien　見　See, 47, 52

chih　之　(possessive), of it, 9, 11, 31, 61, 62, 68, 73, 75, 77
chih　致　Send, attain, 16
chih　知　To know, 28, 33, 56, 70, 71
chih　執　Hold, grasp, 35
chih　至　Reach, become; the extreme, 72
chih　智　Knowledge, 19

ch'in　親　Related, close, favorite, 44, 79

ching　驚　Fear, surprise, 13
ching　靜　Quiet, calm, serene, 37, 45

ch'ing　輕　Lightness, 26
ch'ing　清　Pure, 45

chiu　久　Finally, enduring, 7

ch'u　出　Come out, emerge, 50

ch'u	處	Manage, dwell, 76
ch'ü	曲	Crooked, crippled, 22
ch'üan	全	Whole, complete, 22
chüeh	絕	Sever, banish, end, 19
chung	重	Weight, gravity, 26
ch'ung	冲	To pour, empty, 4
ch'ung	寵	Favor, patronage, 13
erh	而	But, moreover, and, as, 48, 58
fa	法	Rule, law, follow rules, 25
fan	氾	Spread out, overflow, 34
fan	反	Reverse, turn over, opposite, 78
fei	非	No, not, 1
fei	廢	Abolish, reject, 18
hai	海	Ocean, sea, 66
hsi	兮	(pause or exclamation), 20, 21, 34
hsi	希	Few, spare, 23

hsia	下	Falling, lower, under, 17, 29, 45, 46, 61, 67
hsiang	相	Mutually, together, each other, 2
hsiang	祥	Omen, 31
hsiang	象	Elephant; image, 35
hsiao	小	Small, 52, 80
hsien	賢	Virtuous, heroic, 3
hsin	信	Trust, sincere, 49, 81
hsing	行	Walk, move, go, 69
hsiung	雄	Male, hero, 28
hsüan	玄	Mysterious, dark, profound, subtle, 6, 10, 15
hsü	虛	Emptiness, stillness, 16
i	以	By, through, like, with, 11, 37, 54
i	已	End, 30, 55
i	一	One, 42
i	夷	Even, smooth; barbarian, 53
i	易	Easy, simple, 70
jan	然	Certainly, naturally, 23, 25

jen	仁	Kind, benevolent, 5
jen	人	Person, human, 12
jo	若	Resemble; and, if, 8, 13, 78
jo	弱	Weak, frail, 76
jou	柔	Soft, weak, 76
ju	辱	Disgrace, humiliation, 13
ju	如	Like, as, 39
ju	入	Enter, 43, 50
kan	敢	Dare; sad, tragic, 74
ken	根	Root, 26, 59
k'o	可	Possible, can be, 1
ku	故	Therefore, reason, 2, 60, 64
ku	固	Hard, firm, 59
kua	寡	Few, 80
kuang	光	Shine, sparkle, 58
kuei	歸	Return, 60
kuo	國	Country, 80

li 立 Stand, 24

ling 令 Command, cause, 12

lo 落 Fall, drop, scatter, 39

mang 盲 Blind, 12

mei 美 Beautiful, pretty, 81

miao 妙 Wondrous, mysterious, secret, 15, 27

min 民 People, 75, 80

ming 名 Name, 32, 41, 44

ming 明 Bright, illumination, enlightened, 33, 36, 52

ming 冥 Dark, obscure, 21

mu 目 Eye, 12

pai 敗 Defeat, lose, 64

p'in 牝 Female, 6, 61

ping 兵 Soldier, weapon, 31

ping 病 Sick, ill, 71

pu	不	No, not, 3, 5, 24, 30, 31, 37, 38, 48, 55, 56, 58, 68, 71, 73, 81
se	色	Color, 12
shan	善	Good, perfect, 8, 49
shang	尚	Yet, still; honor, glorify, 3
shang	上	Rise up, high, above, best, supreme, 8, 17, 38, 71, 76
shen	神	Spirit, spiritual, 29
shen	身	Body, 44
shen	甚	Very, 53, 70
shen	深	Deep, 59
sheng	生	Birth, existence, originate, 2, 40, 42, 50
sheng	聖	Sacred, learning, 19
shih	是	This, it, 6, 10, 14, 27, 36, 51, 59, 65, 68, 69
shih	石	Stone, rock, 39
shou	守	Defend, guard, 28
shu	孰	Which, where, who, 44, 74
shui	水	Water, 8

szu 死 Death, 50

ta 大 Large, great, 18, 34, 35, 53, 67, 72

t'ai 太 Large, great, 17

Tao 道 Way, road, spiritual path; to say, to tell, 1, 4, 9, 14, 18, 25, 30, 32, 34, 41, 42, 46, 47, 53, 55, 62, 67, 73, 77, 79

Te 德 Virtue, integrity, energy, force, moral power, 10, 38, 49, 51, 60, 65, 68

ti 地 Earth, 5, 7
ti 柢 Root, base, 59

t'ien 天 Heaven, 5, 7, 9, 29, 45, 46, 47, 61, 67, 73, 77, 79

tsao 早 Quick, soon, 30, 55

tse 則 Rule, law; therefore, consequently, 22, 72

t'un 沌 Chaos, confusion, 20

t'ung 通 Through, penetrating, 15

tzu 自 Self, nature, 23, 25, 33

tz'u	此	This, that, 54
tz'u	雌	Female, 28
wan	萬	Ten thousand, man, all, 62
wei	謂	To say, to call, 6, 10, 14, 27, 36, 51, 59, 65, 67, 68, 69
wei	爲	To be, do, cause, act, 11, 26, 45, 48, 57, 63, 64
wei	微	Small, obscure, subtle, dark, 15, 36
wei	事	Thing, 57
wei	威	Authority, power, threat, 72
wo	我	I, my, 57, 67
wu	無	Not have, without, non-being, 2, 11, 31, 40, 41, 43, 48, 57, 63, 64, 69, 79
wu	五	Five, 12
wu	物	Thing, being, 62
wu	吾	I, my, 70
yao	要	Important, vital, 27
yao	燿	Burn, dazzle, 58
yao	窈	Obscure, shadowed, 21
yen	言	Word, talk, 23, 56, 70, 78, 81

yen 焉 In that situation, there; how, where, 60

yin 隱 Retire, hide, 41

yu 有 Have, be, 2, 40, 43, 46

yü 於 In, on, from, 40

yü 與 And, or, 44

yü 欲 Desire, wish, 37

yüan 元 Origin, basic, 51, 65

yüeh 曰 Say, call, 52

yung 用 Use, 11